In Praise of *In a Tension of Leaves and Binding*

Right from the first poem we are taken sometimes like a whirlwind, other times held tenderly in a palm of Mother Nature's hand into a world of leaf and bole, the umwelten of garden, forest and backyard. Sgroi's poems explore the mystery of living organisms we tend to take for granted. This collection makes us consider the world around us and the languages spoken we do not listen to. Renée M. Sgroi is listening.

—**Lynn Tait**, author of *You Break It You Buy It*

This book is a wonder, playing with form and language and stretching the boundaries of what the very best poetry can achieve. These nature-rooted poems, take the ordinary and, through the poet's alchemy, transform the everyday into something magical. This book, dazzles "enough to silver, to shine, gold and chiaroscuro with light." At once erudite and inviting, here is a beautifully written collection of fresh and interesting poems that is as earthy, rich and lush as the gardens Sgroi celebrates.

—**Marsha Barber**, author of *Kaddish for My Mother*

"sweetness is the sound a pen makes / or a spine's crack when first opened / as a birth canal binds daughter, mother / into a book of doubled pages" (from the title poem, "in a tension of leaves and binding"). A poet sits vigil, bears witness and we participate in a cycle of life and death– palpable, visible, quotidian. Led by her questions – "What is a loss?" and "What is a visitation?" – we are visitors in the poet's garden, where animals, plants, soil, rain, replicate, expand, die, revisit. Where the wondrous world continues its exertions regardless of human naming presence. Where we mourn the pain of human loss. Where we celebrate the human birth, our own birth -- like birds irrupting into existence, "bursting in to the room where our lives began" (from "irruptions"). And we participate in this earnest play – to the point of holding book up to mirror, until we realize all the poems are mirrors, we are mirrors, words cast actual shadows, our little lives hold meaning. Thank you, Renée M. Sgroi, for the holy energy with which your fingers caressed this tangled earth of relationships and leaves. With re͞   love.

—**Darlene Madott**, author of *Dying T*

In a Tension of Leaves and Binding

ESSENTIAL POETS SERIES 312

Canada Council **Conseil des Arts**
for the Arts **du Canada**

ONTARIO ARTS COUNCIL
CONSEIL DES ARTS DE L'ONTARIO
an Ontario government agency
un organisme du gouvernement de l'Ont

Guernica Editions Inc. acknowledges the support of the Canada Council
for the Arts and the Ontario Arts Council. The Ontario Arts Council
is an agency of the Government of Ontario.

We acknowledge the financial support of the Government of Canada.

Renée M. Sgroi

In a Tension of Leaves and Binding

GUERNICA
EDITIONS

TORONTO – CHICAGO – BUFFALO – LANCASTER (U.K.)

2024

Guernica Founder: Antonio D'Alfonso

Michael Mirolla, editor
Cover and interior design: Errol F. Richardson

Guernica Editions Inc.
1241 Marble Rock Rd., Gananoque, (ON), Canada K7G 2V4
2250 Military Road, Tonawanda, N.Y. 14150-6000 U.S.A.
www.guernicaeditions.com

Distributors:
University of Toronto Press Distribution (UTP)
5201 Dufferin Street, Toronto (ON), Canada M3H 5T8
Independent Publishers Group (IPG)
814 N Franklin Street, Chicago, IL 60610, U.S.A.

First edition.
Printed in Canada.

Legal Deposit – Third Quarter
Library of Congress Catalogue Card Number: 2024933347
Library and Archives Canada Cataloguing in Publication
Title: In a tension of leaves and binding / Renée M. Sgroi.
Names: Sgroi, Renée M., author.
Series: Essential poets ; 312.
Description: Series statement: Essential poets series ; 312
Identifiers: Canadiana 20240328310 | ISBN 9781771839150 (softcover)
Subjects: LCGFT: Poetry.
Classification: LCC PS8637.G76 I5 2024 | DDC C811/.6—dc23

Contents

systema	11
A mother plants	12
in the garden	13
onion	14
the square of my garden	15
places	17
soil analysis	18
visitations (conformity)	19
class, order, genus, species, variety	20
Cucumis sativus	21
you have called me clay	24
Blue fescue	25
visitations (abundance)	26
Topiary	27
morphology	28
carpenter ants	29
ants (formiche)	30
invasion	31
visitations (scattering)	32
earth	33
heartbreak	34
while reading The New Yorker	35
September grasshopper	36
grasshopper	37
irruptions	40
carrot	41
Multiplier of forms	43
Lumbricus	44

MIXED-METHODS EXPERIMENTAL STUDY OF
ACER SACCHARUM IN SITU, WITH PROGNOSIS

BY ARBORISTS AND LINGUISTS ON THE FUTURE
OF INTERSPECIES COMMUNICATION:
AN INVESTIGATION   45
in a tension of leaves and binding   50
your town   52
visitations (chipping)   53
sparrows   54
preserving tomatoes   55
Solanum lycopersicum   56
sylvilagus floridanus   57
invasion   58
Cucumis sativus   59
irruptions   60
I am the blanket of red-orange leaves   61
Sciuris carolinensis   63
Gestating   64
reincarnate (adj.)   65
différance   66
body singing   69
Danaus plexippus   71
a day is as long as   72
visitations (pompe funebri)   74
weirding   75
exposed   76
apple trees in late winter as if angry   77
hurricane   78
swallow (verb)   79
umbilical   80
wild turkey   81
today the earth is damp with scent   82
visitations (echoes)   83
processing oxygen   85
Water is   87

cucumis sativus   89
rain   91
in metamorphosis   92
thirst   93
wind   95
the winds have come   96
sciuris carolinensis   97
visitations (osso)   99
preparing to overwinter   101
leftover precipitation   102
snow   103
blizzard   104
after the obit   105
the garden sleeps now   106
definition   107
d fin t on   108
and Binding   109

Sources   116
Glossary   117
Acknowledgements   119
About the Author   121

The story begins with the end. Speak or die.
And for as long as you go on speaking, you will not die.
The story begins with death.
    —**Paul Auster,** *The Invention of Solitude*

We
read to inherit the words, but something
is always between us and the words.
    —**Victoria Chang,** *OBIT*

systema

*It is the exclusive property of man [sic], to contemplate and to reason on
the great book of nature.*
—**Carl Linnaeus**, *Systema Naturae, trans.* by William Turton, 1802

let us imbricate ourselves like stories.   a book

sifts pages, weeds out loosestrife , phragmites
ploughs fields like oxen   left to right, right to left
underlines words like *petiole*,   like *phloem*, *xylem* and oxygenates
breath, transcribing *angiosperm*   and *pistil* and *stamen*, with index
finger poised and pointing at   adjectives, traces rabbit warrens,
lies prone on measurement of   a wing's span, travels
length of rain and bears thorax   of a fly

but there is soil on her hands

and stains tomato plants leave, shards of clouded
moonlight, a speck of pollen, wet purple coneflower petals, a band
of spectral blue, the lost scent of lilac, a desiccated insect or
the heat of moths under lamplight

observe the body

as it worms between leaves, squeezes into folio, witness to textured
weave, to signatures bound in faux leather, in paperback, translations
between rows of beans, pods of verbal clauses dangling from stems
while fields lie fallow, forests burn perforated pages where words,
whole paragraphs stack justified in columns, sliced cubes of letters
under crumble of *Pink Pearl* erasers as the system of nature,
like absented rivers, flows unmarked in the margins

A mother plants

her voice like a watermelon

seed we were afraid would grow and stick
in our tummies, large
her tendrils tracing architecture of
lips before our births, before
we knew meanings of words, green
that leads to ripened flesh, flesh
before we knew we were selves
or perceived sun warming bodies,
plants before the feel of the gardener's
touch tending her tender seedlings

    her voice, whether lifting or falling
    her voice, settling the ground for our production
    her voice, a reedy call to the winds

a fibrous muscle to the back fence
our yardstick and our weather vane
our openings and our beginnings
burgeoning into speech
to cries, to screams, to laughter

    and we

    her answer and her unknown chorus   listening

in the garden

so much depends[*]
on your voice, echoed

inside a cracked wheelbarrow
the hollowness

of your tone, tined
and faltering

through a fault
     metal

*from William Carlos Williams, "The Red Wheelbarrow"

onion

I cry, I cry.
stuffed into back garden
like a servant amongst radishes
and buried too too close to beans –
oh for space

how could I be beautiful
as my cousins, daffodils
who buy prime real estate
in flowering pots and beneath
the tall maple by the garden's gate

how can they be blamed? They are
narcissi at any rate, while I
in my shadowed corner grow accustomed
to spiders and to you who wait
to pluck me, to reveal my face

I cry. To be an onion with skin as
thin as paper is a terrible fate

the square of my garden

is a plot x by y in width and depth

to measure means a place is owned,
as i, too have been possessed

grief a five letter word that spells
'intense sorrow', which i imagine
as raindrops that saturate soil,
reach deep into the garden's roots

where i buried mine, dead
tomato stalks, soil
over dried out stems mulched
and put to rest for winter.

decayed plants are deceptive

as grief, which springs, unexpected
as the thyme i thought had suffered
from overwatering, or the onion
that returned the following year
to produce its own bulb

containers construct the necessary coffers for sadness

as a garden retains nutrients, a human iris
a field of scars the body can't relinquish

moss grass, hunter, army, serge, forest, puce, puke,

morphology as a stipule on a stalk after Dionne Brand, here an extent of field:

peacock, shamrock, avocado, sage or like an emerald, jade, fern, string of kelp, seaweed, sea-green,

twig, tawny, umber, cucumber, lime, tea, mint, mango, pea, olive
twisting bark into sienna, ochre, taupe, beige, sand, tan, and walnut
enough to silver, to shine, gold and chiaroscuro with light

places

Places ... are imbricated not only with stories but also with memories.
—**Sarah Wylie Krotz,** *"Place and Memory: Rethinking the Literary Map of*
Canada", English Studies in Canada 40.2-3 (June/September, 2014) pp. 133-154

her stories incline toward fences
and leaves

maple's feet mark perimeters
with textures of winter

stories snatched:

like birds' nests,
dangling modifiers in beaks

squirrels of syntax cross narrative
arcs, infinitives

dried bark and wings
weave twigged mercies

like fairy tales, memorized places
and a quest to take flight

soil analysis

80% shield and strata, 30% backhoe and excavator. 2/3 sand from tropical seas followed by ice ages, in short, too much time spent under water. one part loam, three parts loss and longing. annual tear-filled pints, poured and planted upside down each autumn with bulbs in centimetres of sadness. deposits? innumerable: igneous, metamorphic, covered of course by sedimentary animal scat. minerals. Fe. millimeters (countless) of rain and melted snow. dead leaves. lumens, watts, sunlight kilojoules and their warmth, warmth, warmth. whole parts of at least one known broken heart, scattered shoddily as several kilograms of grass seed. worms (thousands) and fifteen ant hills. larvae (one kind or another) waiting to transform. roots – rhizomatic spread, also those from trees. somewhere toward the core a plate, a crust, magma, an inner fire that burns miles beneath the surface. rocks, cigarette butts, beer bottle caps left behind during house construction. small plastic toys forgotten over winter now very, very slowly (let's call it glacially) degrading. footsteps in the millions: bare, shod, sometimes buoyant. volumes or metres of dreams whispered to the insides of fragile stems and stalks that have since fallen, earthbound. heartbreak, desperation, but also hope, also sustenance, and the holy energy from fingers that can only ever caress ground with reverence

visitations (conformity)

Agelaius phoeniceus,
  Archilocus colubris,
    Cardinalis cardinalis,
      Carduelis pinus,
        Carduelis tristis,
          Carpodacus mexicanus,
            Carpodacus purpureus,
              Corvus brachyrhyncos,
                Junco hyemalis
                  Larus delawarensis
                    Passer domesticus
                      Poecile atricapilla,
                        Quiscalus quiscula,
                          Spizella passerina,
                            Spizella pusilla, Sturnus vulgaris,
                              Turdus migratorius Zenaida
                              macroura

class, order, genus, species, variety

Linnaeus mapped hierarchies based on stamens and pistils, forgetting roots, seeds, flowers or fruits, a process which must have appealed to you, ordering species, plucking one genus from another into rearranged parts, binomial varieties: girl, boy, parent, child, friend, not-so-friendly, kind, pain in the ass. classifications bleeding into bloodstream the way a god created Eve in the second version from Adam's rib, her body dragging behind the oxen cart a never-ending game of catch-up, all the while children spilling from her womb inscribing generations under writ not hers, though she lived by it. how you accepted that storied tale and fed it to us, like stuffed peppers, tomato sauce and olive oil oozing at burnt edges. those that followed Linnaeus changed the script as also i'll conceptualize you, differently now, wish for you a cross-pollination, new species, genus, a means to open categories, reorder sequences, add variety to classes, and write books which you could read, at bedtime, to unborn children

Cucumis sativus

cold

wet

warmer

white-grey

sunlight   stubble

serrated edges

ser - rated

stalks

stubble   leaves

stubble

tendrils   stubble   yellow

flowers   on

fruit   thick-skinned

                                                                    fruit

                                                          stalks

          tendrils

     curl, curl,   curl stake   curl
                   stubble petiole,   funnel

          stubble   water

                                   water   water water water
trellis   fence   pole

   water   water   fly

light
water   water   leaves leaves flower

               insect   worms
flower

stubble   water
flower

                                                           unfurl

          curl

fruit   squirrel fruit   fruit   insect
                   squirrel

stubble   stubble   flower
                                                    fruit

water   water
              sunlight

                    sssssssseeeeeeeeeeeeeeeeeeeeeeeeds

you have called me clay

have pierced me with your spade

have called me porous, pumice-like, dissembling
beneath surface, beneath sand

what is visible resides in water
that filters above shoulders. I soak in moisture

like a dried-out lake, you receded.
I begged you not to leave, but the sun and

the moon and the cold and the heat, indeed heat.

you have called me powder,
have called me shallow

with dampened eyes I break
as shale breaks, single slice by alternate

slice you dig. you grow furrows on your brow

how you enlarge the pit of me

my heart rolls, over
eyes turned from wandering clouds

Blue fescue

we were holding insects
holding a space for weeds for
we were not so thick as not to permit
intruders

our seeds in flower, their delicate
petals small, shy
requiring your special lens
to see them

our hair was long, and only then
did you observe our blades
for we are cutting, serrated
but in your eyes in need of a trim

your straight edge against concrete
curbing our sidewalk reach
a measuring and a tapering

we were as a field, as

a human body a field primed,
shaved by your shaping

visitations   (abundance)

Archilocus colubris   Agelaius phoeniceus,

, , Cardinalis cardinalis   Carduelis pinus,

Carduelis tristis,   Carpodacus mexicanus,

Carpodacus purpureus,   Corvus brachyrhyncos,

Junco hyemalis,

Larus delawarensis,   Passer domesticus,

Poecile atricapilla,   Quiscalus quiscula,

Spizella passerina,   Spizella pusilla,

Sturnus vulgaris,   Turdus migratorius,

Zenaida macroura

Topiary

a conifer, perhaps a pine
and trimmed
to live its life inside
a shape of needles

the way we landscape selves
into globes, fanciful rabbits,
prune ourselves to fit
within a pigeon framed
as dove

and pulled from magic hat
the trick of it, of scissors
and of shears, the tree
stands silent through its
summer, through its years

silenced, a conifer hedged
can't hold the birds, its boughs
too slender and
too thinned
to bear anything
              but light

morphology

Use care when measuring out book, setting pages, selecting glue for perfect binding and plotting spots for seeds and the right amount of shade to host a trillium. Add compost and fresh soil to vegetable bed, investing nitrogen-rich ingredients to feed hunger of a story. Fences are often posted before arrivals, so be wary of parameters. Your story will include hail but not enough snow. Occasionally breezes rustle leaves, and peace must be made with Virginia creeper. Every story begins somewhere, and the geology of sandy soil suggests water. There may be a farm but any trace of apple roots or cattle should be scraped like palimpsests. Add tension and point fingers at weeds, squirrels or mice for eating at your pages. Narrators can be unreliable, so set letters carefully to avoid triggering some unrest. If you wish to articulate antagonists, speak them into arguments over perennials or shrubs. Your book should lie open like a photo album on coffee table, but remember that photographs record in two dimensions. Add the texture of heavy bond. New characters may be intrusive, but excise these else you will struggle with an ending.

carpenter ants

have sawed into the fence —
the post's top, once symmetrical
possessed of a flat lip,
a perfect square overhanging
the long rectangle of column
is now chewed, as if
sucked in with uncertainty,
with self-devouring

chewed and broken, as all
that humans create, breaks:
the cement poured to hold the post
is cracked, the fence leans south
against the weight of wind
and the carpenters, who fashion
a vision of the living world,
nest in the sawed and the pressed
and the pressurized wood
defy human efforts
with their gnashing

ants (formiche)

legs on trunk. tree trunk sized by legs. place. in
the square of garden. food search shelter. in an
anthill, each. colonies, settlements, battalions.
jobs. birth. what is birth? emerging from egg, sac
of eggs, the stickiness. explore. circle. tree bark.
fastidiously. antennae over terrain, aerial mapping.
food. we will march even to branches. lines,
formation. nests beneath soil, beneath shadows.
leaves. surreptitiously. food as is thorax as are
legs. multiples, but not six. six weaves. what is a
sky? circle, square. is a fissure, quashed into earth.
measuring. shelter feed. knot in bark, wood planks.
colonies to settlements to building. nest, tunnel.
tunnel to maze to labyrinth. single file between
one terrain and the next. territorial. two by two
by two by two. each a place, birth emerging from
stickiness. spot of moss on bark. apple scab. green
on grey. lichen. three-dimensional. single file.
tree trunk. legs. cadre of legs. food and shelter.
multiple leaves and a sinew of bark. maze, tunnel,
nest. labyrinthine. colonies. each a spot. circle, tree
trunk, antennae. twitching over knot, over bark

invasion

the news zooms in, a close-up
of an ant's head, its horror
maw menaced by yellow hairs
curled on the chin, angry
as curmudgeon stubble. if i were an ant,
i'd also be peeved, to peer up
from ground level at concrete
monstrosity dwellings humans drop
as if from air onto prime soil – maddening.
i've wondered if it hurts to mark
a chemical scent, to drag across wet leaves
the weight of your body. the middle
of an ant corpse is thorax.
i've set my share of traps, loosed
poison powder onto vulnerable corners
in summer when the ants crawl in.
they always crawl in.
but who can blame them, the attempt
to trek up lengths of legs or crowd
food morsels en masse – we can't
tidy our messes. i don't fear the photo,
and i'm not ashamed of my crimes.
wouldn't you raise your fists if you were hungry?
if your land was invaded by aliens?

Note: the poem refers to the photo taken by Eugenijus Kavaliauskas of Lithuania, and published in the article, "A Face Only A Mother Could Love: Terrifying Photo Shows What an Ant Looks Like Up Close" by Zoe Sottile, Oct. 22, 2022, CNN, https://www.cnn.com/style/article/ant-face-close-up-scn-trnd/index.html

visitations (scattering)

pinus

Archilocus
colubris   Larus
Corvus

purpureus   colubris
,   mexicanus,   cardinalis,   Larus
Corvus   Corvus
purpureus

mexicanus
pinus   macroura
vulgaris
Archilocus   Corvus
Atricapilla   Poecile
cardinalis

domesticus   purpureus
vulgaris   vulgaris   hyemalis
macroura   atricapilla   Junco
tristis tristis   tristis

passerina, Turdus,   Poecile,   Carpodacus,   Carduelis
Sturnus
Qui-scalus

Cardinalis
Agelaius,   Quiscalus,   Cardinalis
tristis   Zenaida   Atricapilla

Junco
Sturnus.   migratorius,   tristis, domesticus,   Zenaida
migrat-orius   migratorius pusilla,
phoeniceus,   delawarensis,   brachyrhyncos
phoeniceus   Sturnus   Quis calus
Domesticus   phoeniceus   phoeniceus   phoeniceus
Passer   Passer   Passer

earth

how you bulldozed me, ripped

me of flesh
inside   in   out, tied
wilds i'd inherited from myself,

bruises beneath bark, lies seeding the saltiness of oceans

my protuberances you chopped
math-like, adding up to
this one and this one and
this,   lost

reaping my fecundity

settling city after
city, subway turnstiles
like animals, toxic
mix of methane and atmosphere.

evening brings the rain
of corrosive flakes
the world is mapped by the streams
of murderous chemicals

and the riverbeds, receptacles
where contaminants sleep,
snug as bedbugs, between strata

heartbreak

splits the horizon

as dawn does, into beginning day
like a beat mid-sentence, fibrillating.

the past tense of break is broke
which a heart never is

never broken into like a bank that masquerades
as a fortress, but is robbed of its currency.

instead, a heart shatters like a blue vase
knocked, a door that opens

onto chambers where the echoes can't account
for a pulse, where bloodied feet cut themselves

on the shards of azured reflections.

a hairline fracture traces fault lines before a break,
reveals breakage built into bone.

a heart is said to be muscular,
it is rather a shell, bi-valve

enclosing itself, accreting
into the purchase of morning where dawn

that precious commodity, waits,
crepuscular, iridescent

while reading *The New Yorker*

you learn that Staten Island is overrun by deer. they trespass highways without paying tolls, for what is a crossing after all but a chance to escape the ferryman? you contemplate that myth as your head inclines towards the window; the street's resident raccoon reigns as sure as squirrels scurry again to attics where they build more nests. these aren't ordinary thefts, these mammalian invasions, setting, settling their lives in dumpsters and housing units as hallmarks, signposts like lowered drawbridges into what we call civilization. no, they are as spring-loaded traps that bait citizens so that we square-off surrounding wildlife, two halves split by the unmarked river we refuse to name, the river we claim defines boundaries. being boxed-in necessitates improvisation, as a jazz riff that loosens, links against limits, which the trespassing deer understand having no respect for taxation. and those of us who have crossed over live together in a legend, key to any map's comprehension, synanthropes in the labyrinth of our habitation

*The article referenced in the poem is "Deer Wars and Death Threats" by Brooke Jarvis, *The New Yorker*, November 15, 2021 issue

RENÉE M. SGROI

September grasshopper

all throughout you have been
leaping from rock to rock and
from blade to blade as if your only
concern is to entertain nearby children

they play in the street, their bikes
and toys strewn across lawns
abandoned for some new pursuit
a game of hide and seek for
they are nowhere seen except
in their summer remnants

and in futile attempts to catch
you in homemade traps, their season
for make-believe, for leaving
bats and balls and skipping ropes
in the grass where you jump
and stridulate, and like you

September brings its frantic fall leap
to the unknown generations late spring
will greet

I crouch down, close to the earth—
your multiplexing eyes make
a kaleidoscope of me

grasshopper

in jumping,   i jump

jump

rock to blade, blade past foot

jump

hide in green grass

                        chew, chew

jump

stop.   listen –

still body trembles
eye the large bird

                        wait. wait.

                              then

jump

bird hops

                    no match

jump

                                        bold my strides
                                          lengths ahead

        jump

                                        notice,
                                          stridulate

        female in low tree

        jump close
stridulate,   she bends

        jump

                                        soon, soon

                                        catch as she passes

        she

                        jumps

                                        another mate

        jump

another

jump

day

irruptions

The departure of the birds from their normal range is an eruption, but their arrival somewhere else is the reverse – an irruption, a bursting in
—**Scott Weidensaul**, *Living on the Wind: Across the Hemisphere with Migratory Birds*

long after i had grown and found myself
a mother of small child, when i lived my first

domestic life in another home, a November
owl landed on our back fence in rain

perhaps lost, its young compass skewed

the owl, irrupting in the way children
push through their parents' bedroom door

as once on Christmas, the year our dad
remained upstairs recuperating

and we celebrated spiritual birth on the bed
where like birds we irrupted into existence

bursting in to the room where our lives began

carrot

and I shall put forth eyes in the darkness of soil,
shall be seen unto those who dwell with me

I shall array my fronds and my yellowed roots,
soft as the fur the rabbit leaves by, seeding.

my greens shall harness sun,
shall grow tall in its direction,
transmitter of light and radiant nutrience

I shall photosynthesize,
unlock the genes of one hundred and fifty steps,
transform protein to beta-carotene.

therefore shall I remain,
deep in the shelter of my sheltering

and I shall stretch, bend unto the arms of earth, and the earth
with gladness shall open a space to receive me.

I shall release all my incongruities.

nothing below or above the surface of soil shall harm me:
not insect, not rodent, nor insufficient depth.

I am not withdrawn.
I am as flesh unto flesh unto flesh in this darkness of soil.

I am reserved, for though the human hand
shall disrupt me, I grow purple, orange

rain shall wash the ends of my fronds
and wet my surfaces

I, too shall be doused with the wonder of meaning

I shall drink all water, for lo,
I shall not suffer from thirst nor drowning

the soil is my sponge
verily, I shall not drown.

the onions and marigolds and those
who grow around me shall observe:

envy this coolness,

this soil which sticks to my skin, this skin
which so firmly holds the heart of me in place

I shall not fear the squirrel's riven glance
for it senses not the scent of orange

Multiplier of forms

September in the damp of morning and i contemplate worms:

how Amphioxus' notochord evolved, and sits between our vertebrae,
like a vermiform appendix tying us to itself, blind

how evolution of cell after cell splitting becomes
more wondrous than a maker's blueprint could imagine

how a worm's body re-collects, if severed,

turns earth brown, unimaginative as if worms exist
to feed birds and fish, have no need of beauty for themselves

how they wriggle in the rain,
equilibrium between moisture and flooding a fine one.

how we too must live in the balance of heat and water

like worms, stepping lightly over dried ones,
covering with soil those dug up while planting

a sunflower, around which earth spins,
angled axis churns, connects to soil, to the worm

that somewhere in the garden prepares for equinox

Lumbricus

robins persist, and we're defenceless
in rain

a wriggled life is this

lived in the cool and damp
reaching for light and
drowned by deluge

some survive but only just
some die under blade
some destroyed by shovel.
we have seen those too

their remains mark pavement
sun's asphyxiation a drowning.

who mourns lost loves?

much loss is followed by much wiggling,
water life force and detriment

we,
transform invisible selves
tasked to render the earth

MIXED-METHODS EXPERIMENTAL STUDY OF *ACER SACCHARUM* IN SITU, WITH PROGNOSIS BY ARBORISTS AND LINGUISTS ON THE FUTURE OF INTERSPECIES COMMUNICATION: AN INVESTIGATION

Abstract:

This paper seeks to investigate. As a tree, a log, as so much bark, sawdust. Dyes and additives. Colours and glue. Characters and looped letters. To learn how to adhere to the sides of other pages.

Introduction:

This study originated with the unanticipated discovery of a fragment of speech buried deep within a recently deceased and ancient *acer saccharum*. Notified by local lumberjacks or also bark harvesters, the principal investigators (PIs) rushed to the site to capture said fragment before dissipation (fragment reproduced in its roughest translation below). As a result of this unexpected quarry, PIs assembled a team to examine the range of possible utterances.

Once, I was a seedling, and I fell. A beautiful fall, though it was spring. Few observe where a seedling lands. I was cracked and therefore open. Such is the art of germination. First there is a sapling, then a tree. A process depends on so much light and a little rain. To become tree means to offer life: insects, birds, squirrels, raccoons. Oxygen.

Falling is an element like carbon.

Methods:

"To make paper from trees, the raw wood has to be turned into pulp. This pulp is made up of wood fibers and chemicals that are mixed together. They can either be processed mechanically or chemically. With mechanical pulping, machines grind wood chips into pulp. The fibers are ground down more in this process, so the paper that is made is not as strong. This kind of paper is commonly used for newsprint and phone books." [1]

For the purposes of our research, we consulted with two differentiated manufacturers of coloured paper. Said manufacturers also produce glues and other adhesives. We consulted with a grove of trees. Their response was, needless to say, wooden.

"The second, and more commonly used, method is chemical pulping. Chemical pulping creates stronger paper, since this method eliminates most of the natural glue-like substance in the pulp."[2]

Removing glue, and later adding it. To stack pages together, to adhere to walls. To render the world of human ideas visible, intransient. To be ringed into binders, coils, duo-tangs, cerlox, loose-leafed in thin plastic shrink-wrap. To sit in blocks on kitchen counters. To be wrapped in more paper and put through a machine called printer. But first to become pulp. To be mashed, drained of life-bearing water. Drowned, the water in your veins replaced by chemicals.

"Once the paper has about 50 percent of its water removed, it is heated to dry to between 5 and 8 percent water content. At this point, the paper may go through treatments to create different textures. It is then wound into a reel. These reels of paper are so large that large cranes have to be used to move them."[3]

Dry -ing.   s.......s.......s......
yllables

The PIs conducted numerous experiments in forests of *acer saccharum* using recording devices capable of capturing high and low frequencies (beyond the range of human hearing), and the thinnest of whispers. Samples and measurements on the health and viability of subjects for this study (excluding rings counted) were acquired. Experiments included phrases spoken in multiple languages by linguist team members at a variety of pitches and decibels to ascertain subject response. Forest bathing was avoided, as the researchers concluded this practice would not be conducive to interspecies communication on the basis of the absence of utterances.

Results:
Captured on closed-circuit television. Here, the song of a dying leaf:

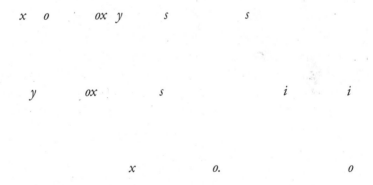

Our research findings have uncovered whole libraries of paper. Bound as books between leather covers, although often pressboard or thickened sheets of paper and shelved in alpha-numeric systems as archive, repository. As devices, to be opened or closed at will, at the discretion, desire of the human hands for which they were produced, for which they fit neatly into.

It is worth remarking that while libraries are not portable, individual units are. The PIs collected several volumes as specimens, and are studying them further in the lab. A separate paper is soon to be published on their conclusions. What follows outlines key preliminary data from their findings:

Some books have markings, in pencil, coloured pencil, even pen. Torn off covers. Folded edges replete with strips of coloured paper. Chewed or inflexible spines. Pages that are wont to escape from bindings as autumn leaves from a tree.

Discussion:
Trees imbibe words, weather, beverage stains. Literary canons or possibly integers. Banish the defecated. Bleed anapests or dactyls. Manifestos as reason or unreason. Drink in wax crayons, watercolours, remains of lunch or groceries. Parking tickets. Build boats, docks, bridges, skeletons of houses. Play board games, baseball, cricket, croquet. Invite recipes, birthdays, late slips. Turn backs of sympathy notes or envelopes with numbers. Embody fences, shade avenues. Tree products, paper products. Produced, producing, productive. Pulp. Sawdust. Tissues and the 3-ply salt-heat of tears. Lignans made manifest. Or something called human. Intelligence.

```
chop          buzz         rrrwwww        whirr        grind
      sweep         mash          churn         churn        vlet
glong         stretch      vlak            wrap         shake
dry           rattle            snap              truck      stack
throw         chunk        blank          balump
rattle
```

silence   .

stain	*wipe*	*soak*	*bleed*	*hang*
crumple	*cold*	*stink*	*fold*	*mash*
churn	*stretch*			

Conclusions:

Both arborists and linguists maintain a poor and limited prognosis on interspecies communication based on research findings.

Notes:

1 "How Paper is Made from a Tree" (n.d.), available at: https://www.treeremoval.com/how-paper-is-made-from-a-tree/

2 "How Paper is Made from a Tree" (n.d.), available at: https://www.treeremoval.com/how-paper-is-made-from-a-tree/

3 "How Paper is Made from a Tree" (n.d.), available at: https://www.treeremoval.com/how-paper-is-made-from-a-tree/

in a tension of leaves and binding

there is bark.　　a spine clasp,
like a ring of stitches,

glues that bandage stories
only the dried grass remembers

in a tension, a book is bound
verso, recto,

like a mother
facing pages her daughter traces, then erases

a mother, daughter could scrape their skins

like vellum, remove marks of bristles
but their knives would collect blood,

their residual blades would glisten.

in a tension of leaves, a flyleaf photo
offers credit, a type of ownership

printed in italics, which is a slant
read in every vein of leaf, of stoma

that breathes life into a transverse
seedling that falls, like a daughter

under the spell of limbs
and recto verso, inscribes a flower

an emblem, imprimatur
stamped green with chlorophyll,

with the sunlight it transforms into sugars.

sweetness is the sound a pen makes
or a spine's crack when first opened

as a birth canal binds daughter, mother
into a book of doubled pages

and into the sweep a willow branch extends
low beside the river,

and snaps

in a tension of leaves and binding,
a daughter and her mother meet

somewhere beneath the tree's cast shadow,
between the turning motion thumb and index make

before the paper decays, acid-based,
into the act of kerning

your town

where i didn't see swallows

dip, their forked tails as
the river

diverted, and how the stream's interment
gutted the place, smooth metres of
tongue-like lava flows of concrete
covering water, slicing
down through this half
of town and that, mute

ripples once laughed
under swan dives by
birds, their round nests under eaves
language curves
uccello, rondinello

swallow a failure of terms

a return

to throat
to drink from your
rechannelled river, and

the parchedness of it

visitations (chipping)

chipping   *house*   *dove*

robin

      robin   *chickadee*   *finch*

starling   *cardinal*

     starling   *sparrow*

    sparrow   *icterid*   *gull*

              gull

      sparrow

gull gull gull gull   *crow*

       sparrow

                 crow

    goldfinch

    goldfinch   *chipping*   *house sparrow*

    purple finch

mourning   *house sparrow*

sparrows

wing into the lilac, three on a branch
and i wonder if we appear lifeless, large,
a middle-aged couple intruding
on survival, its transactions
of this branch or that, and
the competition over mates

they are house sparrows, these three
that scare a pair of cardinals intent
on nesting in the ninebark,
the cardinals' flick of combs like licks of flame

the smaller birds are unafraid to extinguish.

unfailing, the trio claims the shrub

for their menage à trois,
or so we imagine, limited
as we are by our own sense of space

we increase the distance between us
for the silence that occupies it

and i wonder if the birds could tell us
their accounts, or if we would listen

preserving tomatoes

i'd watch you slice one like a heart

rows and rows of tomatoes, dried
on basement blankets like sleeping children

in your hands two halves
open, bleeding. sometimes you'd
dig out seeds, buckets filling
like bronchioles learning to breathe

we were redness

strained of skins, apprenticed to
mastery of short blades

techniques handed down
like a surgery

Solanum lycopersicum

my wet wet flesh

fattens

skin ripens under synesthetic sun

under leaves, fragrant

that pierce and etch tending hands
who try to stake me

I am

fruit of your passions

kiss

your mouth and tongue

satiating

sylvilagus floridanus

in a hole in the earth, we sleep,
the soft pink flowers and the whitish ones

the bitterness of green stalks

stalks spring up everywhere, the safest, sweetest
shoots, shadows under shrubs

our sister, cousin birthed babies in a tall wood box,
human hands blue-gloved handling young ones

babies not returned to their birth place
our nieces, uncles moved to lesser human spaces

a human reclines on moving seat near our nephew, brother
like the human, he stretches out, dozes drowsily

where the grass is rich, grows in a mass the opposite of dryness

in winter we huddle beneath earth, beneath snow
sleeping, winter is less long

waking, winter a field of harshness

some do not emerge or forage or chew the bark of trees
above cold white crystals. we emerge, brown fur in sun

we have not learned the trick of changing colours

emerging is like sleeping, we succumb to death

on summer evenings, a quietness, crickets and
an invitation to dine on sumptuous dandelion, but quickly

invasion

the spot on the lawn where the spruce once stood
now overrun by ants. they clamber and fall
into my gloves as i plant bulbs, biting.

there was nothing to do but fell the rusted tree.
my saw too small and my skills too poor
for much else but gnawing. how i hacked

at dying limbs and trunk, how the saw's teeth
chattered thunderclaps until all that was left
of blue was a stump.

Nonno was a logger, he scaled
hills above his town, chopped
chestnut, though he must also have sought

other, precious woods. when i knew him,
he was deciduous. hunched in a chair,
his arms and legs trembled with Parkinson's.

my children don't believe me when i say
our ancestors settled atop spindly points
in Calabrian hills to avoid invasion.

invincible youth can't fathom fear, but
after all it is human to hide our nests.
what skill my Nonno possessed

felling trees was not passed to me.
my hands upset the rule of ants. they wield
strength in numbers and mandibles, incising

Cucumis sativus

I glare at my lover the sun

why have I been left to die, submit to my own decay?
I asked to grow, perform my duties,
turn green my prickles.

the squirrels. birds peck

my seeds burst but find no fertile ground

I am open, ancient. Observe my skin:

to melt is also my duty, to allow my flesh to fester
to a universe of flies that attend my wake.   they drone.
bees buzz, their words of no consequence

I am solitary

and while I grew, I grew apart, greeted only by
the earth that expected me, the air and soft rain
that caressed my cheek.

my flesh is speckled now,
and should a worm, a crawling insect slide its way to sleep
inside me should I be content?
be leased to those who would rent

space inside my peel?   my walls are cavernous cool,
made lucid by spent green that yet surrounds them

like you, I am a comfortable bed.

I shed my skin to the wandering skies

59

irruptions

American

                         chipping

              mourning

                  cardinal   *sparrow*

   gull   *crow*

                                robin

                    finch   *finch*

    sparrow

                          purple

   dove   *house*

         goldfinch   *black-capped*   *blackbird*

                       icterid

                         European   *thrush*

 starling

       chickadee

                   junco   *red-winged*

I am the blanket of red-orange leaves

and the tree.

We fall at your feet, leaves

dress me in skirts for I was always feminine.

I change with each season

stretch my arms bare with
bangles of snow and ice

Spring melts these scenes

denuded as new bird, blind
my body vulnerable

when green summer simmers heat
then I grow out my hair, long

and with passion shake tresses free in thunder.
in the saturated colours above grass I grow

weary, blue-green rain aches but I am
sated by the savour of water.

there is a story to which I am privy,
I open my book: words

fall as meditations from
Marcus Aurelius, august and

October-desiccating. I tie knots

their threads, loose ends are, to me
storied, while you, absorbed

by renderings rake leaves, my clearings

Sciuris carolinensis

bury me under heavy snow and not by the road: I too
have seen my likeness flattened there, decaying. or bury
me beneath a tree, tall limb to my shortened appendages,
heart larger than myself that is the meaning of soul. bury
me beside your garden where you grew such delicious
tomatoes that were my right to steal and leave half eaten. I
make no apologies for you were not born to scurry across
rooftop shingles or feel cold climb each spindly shaft of
fur on a tail. bury me instead under dead leaves newly
fallen, so that all colours your eyes see become my nation's
flag. you will forget to name my existence but the birds
will forever call me predator. bury me up against your
wooden fence, for even then I am close to a tree's splinters.
but do not bury me within the old growth forest thinking
you have blessed me with my habitat, for you will one day
raze that space to pour concrete and my body, like yours,
is meant for the scavenging worms

Gestating

nine months your worm
has sat inside my belly
slowly divesting itself of its silk
unravelling a stretch of cloth
embroidered with your name.

i felt a twinge, a kick
a start before first trimester
my world measured out in threes,
i hand-fed you

leaves, surveyed your cocoon slip
from beneath your feet
sick and nauseous watching
your hieroglyph shrink.

there is a mummy, museumed
disemboweled and camphored.
its visitors gawk and walk away
in horror that a worm could root inside
a woman's womb.

a seed is not a child nor is a worm
a bird. you asked to take flight
emerge from my gut golden
as a word

but after nine months' gestation
i am left with ultrasound in sepia:
an image of a scarab
rolls dung into the earth

reincarnate *(adj.)*

i am certain i had gills, all my life breathing waves,

the scales of my fish body pulsing
like gelid breaststrokes in a murk of marshy water

unsteady legs, bolstered by ill-fitting shoes, feet awake
i inhaled, reeds entering lungs,

was careful of the piercings.

you may not have been a fish
but it's true, you too were once a tadpole

flicking your tail in ultrasound's brackish lagoons

when you found yourself landed, in your hands
pots and spoons, a battery of drums on seafoam laminate.

like this, we become swimmers, reincarnate,
returning to spawn ourselves, where the water meets rocks.

in a school's playground i once witnessed lindens,
leaves like light rippling water

*différance**

there you sit, as do i
in our rooms, at our desks
(possession part of rational equation)
at café tables, in borrowed library carrels,
makeshift drafts contingent upon
wobbly subway train laps, the point
always to seat ass in chair, observe

                        fingers typing
or gripped in the act of futuring writing's
clinical instruments, objectives
antiseptic scalpel culls of lead and ink
that plough page, hear mouth
speak thoughts into cellular mics,
recording tongues equally adept
at drawing lines with sharpened edges.

                        do you recall
grade school primers tracing alphabets
across-field between one pink line,
one blue, gendered tinge of his and hers
inscribed beyond dotted median in
curve of a capital letter?

yes, you at your laptop ensconced, i
with my pen, hack at overgrown thickets
words jumped like terrified grasshoppers'
leaps, looking for higher, safer branches,
adaptations Darwin surely recorded,
natural selection magnifying lens
of imperialism

like my mother,
scrutinizing our hands, we called her
'little Napoleon' because she was short
but commanding her Sunday mass seat
in the front pew where congregants sat
singing *This is the day, this is the day that
the Lord has made* a world in seven days
and on the eighth it was written

in letters, envelopes
trimmed in striped airmail wedges
papercuts of memories meta-morphed
into what we write, unearth as etymologies
search for derivatives, next breath poses
this question

which perhaps you too ask
at your desk, under pools of electric brilliance
or caffeinated reflection, is it as Derrida has it
différance of freedom and domination
loosened tongue as armed subject, vocabulary

of collective weapon, shield of mind
regulating in performative traces, reading
requisites, prerequisites, postrequisites
training right or left hand, scripts as conscripts
to scientific systems anatomical as Saussurean parole

that near the end chains us
to our desks like Linnean classifications
marking butterfly wings as species, lepidoptera
Latin and moth bound?

*The concept of *différance* was postulated by French poststructuralist philosopher Jacques Derrida, who wrote that "Differance is not simply active (any more than it is a subjective accomplishment); it rather indicates the middle voice, it precedes and sets up the opposition between passivity and activity" (p. 385) in Rivkin, J. and Ryan, M. (eds.) (1998) *Literary Theory: An Anthology.* Oxford: Blackwell. For more on Derrida and poststructuralism, see Rivkin and Ryan.

body singing

for all this time, i have been
writing to the cell

you know, the solitary one
that takes up space in

> the empty chair
> the vacant field
> the dreams of forests filled
> with mist and shushing trees

as in me, it's in you

in the distance from rib to
rib, in the hollow the collar bone
cups, fusing to the scapula

the cell sits, in the length of femur
to tibia, heavy-boned,
as a constant, wearing a weary smile.

for all this time, i have been
writing to breathing cities

seeking occupants in
tarsals and metatarsals
seeking twists of wind the ulna

makes when it breaks.   tall cities
stacked, on top of one another
like panes of brittle glass

i have been writing to the building
blocks, the proteins
deoxyribonucleic acids, they

beat hemoglobin, blood.   they travel
roads to city's heart, and leak

through valves that open
systole, diastole

i have been writing to hips, to perpendiculars

of gravity against the children
i bore

the angles we hold against
one another like bricks,
creating barriers

i have been writing to my
heartache, mine or to yours

searching for a field, green
where two chairs sit

vacant, parallel, face forward
like open eyes

Danaus plexippus

my journey long,   they say
my span precise, my speed
so fast. of course, we break along the way

along the way I left my children somewhere
behind a bush in Texas, Vermont, I can't remember
where, we fly in droves, in danger from trucks and cars
people with nets who catch us

my great-great aunt was pinned between pages
of a book a man thought to write, he called us regal
and beside my aunt, wrote: beautiful
despite through sex she'd lost her colour

a book like a wing that flaps but takes
no flight unless it's thrown and even then
its path is short and indirect, bumps up against walls
and lands with a thud

I write. journeys through strands of milkweed

a day is as long as

the length of a day, any day, before a dies irae,
before a long day, today, another day, as wide as a ten-centimetre
wingspan, open, monarch butterfly mid-flight, oyamel firs that wait as if
opening arms, offering warm air deposits

or is a day as long as a length of days, dies irae,
day of the dead, any day death has a day, is a day, sounds wide as a
wingspan, a monarch opens, mid-flight, an oyamel fir awaits, as an
oriole waits

open mouthed, butterflies receive warm air
deposits a kilometre above the ground is not too far to fly, a column, a
corridor, a grosbeak or an oriole on a day of death, swallowing

is as a day as long as a corridor, a column,
monarch wingspans colouring a forest of firs, oyamel, a butterfly is a
death is a wingspan up to ten centimetres on a day as death is a dies
irae

a day of wrath is a day of the dead is an oyamel,
fir dead is a flight, a path a corridor of wingspans, collection of
warm air deposits or column of centimetres colouring of oriole is as
grosbeak is

death is a flight path, today, any day, another
day is a deposit as oriole or grosbeak, swallowing

a monarch butterfly is a flight path is a
wingspan is a corridor a kilometre above the ground is a dead relative
who returns on the day of the dead, butterflies as collections as days
before death before dies irae

swallowing, is a day a wingspan, is an open mouth mid-flight, warm air deposit, monarch is a death is a bird in flight, dies irae is a grosbeak is an oriole is as an oyamel fir waits, open arms

is a day of death, today, any day is as long as a mid-flight wingspan, is as short as ten centimetres, is the length of a kilometre above oyamel firs, is a breath of warm air stopped in the act of swallowing   is

visitations (pompe funebri)

robin   ghiandaia

jay   merlo, merlo
passero

storno   gull gull gull
gabbiano   pichi
jay
corvo   gabbiano
gabbiano   pichi

robin
ghiandaia   miimii   finch
pettirosso

sparrow
ghiandaia   corvo
finch
miimii   uccello
gwiingwiish
uccello
uccello   passero
gyaashkshenh
uccello
pettirosso
gwiingwiish   storno
gwiingwiish
ghiandaia   corvo   corvo
merlo   gabbiano
storno
gyaashkshenh   gabbiano

uccellino, ino, ino   ino

aceddhu   -ddhu   -ddhu

weirding

the fact of a blizzard has not deterred the birds. they return as if spring were a signal to be attended, a flipped channel. on television a scientist speaks of Texas snow as weather weirding, and it is weird, falling too in Athens, in Rome, weird the way snow clings to the side of a wood fence, missing the point of gravity. from this view, snowflakes act like insects, dart around one another, sentient. we used to spin like that, catch them on our outstretched tongues, allow the snow to speak for us with a kind of buzzing. then we were alive, though we buried ourselves in make-believe ice castles, our laughter ringing out against wintry silences. a teacher once said snow was quiet and i listened to it fall, hearing nothing. the birds, ears inside their heads, must hear something other than silence, something weird that calls them back despite the blast of snowflakes, before insects circle in the night around exposed light. snow, transmission like static airwaves on palm and yucca leaves, on dry horizons, vibrating cold and speaking

exposed

January snow sticks to the wind-side of bark –
anneals lignans. stripped of roughness, cold
films maple's clear syrup. how bare
precipitation's clasp of oaks gums
wet crystals, how their edges flake, fuse,
fix six-sides to elm trunks, negative
one Celsius ice-glue captures
beech branch in the stop bath of snowfall.
like a crisp apple cut by stone-whet paring knife,
like a stamp on a body born in a blizzard, like
a lightning-quick scan, water frozen to glass frames,
trees winter. wild hares scurry through depth hoar,
in relief imprints surface. a naked eye like a twig
snaps. an old zirconium foil Magicube flash
explodes, floodlights undersides of limbs

apple trees in late winter as if angry

gnarl, train limbs to knot over trunks,
shuttle spikes skyward, as if a god
wrested darkness to imprint
on trees, exposed
hurt onto bark like a stain.
a is for agon,
for a god who plants green
serpents, of course fork-tongued,
because blossoms eventually fall,
because roundness is enviable.
like wizened Medusas, branches
bear snow, as if to berate
a world that asks them to twist.
fixed on their axes, apple
trees peel-wrap flesh,
so prone to bruising,
to stigmata

hurricane

where we live inland the garden meets the tail end of hurricanes:

a sudden drop in late summer heat and rainfall, heavy, from clouds
that before a single bead marks windows, signal danger

yesterday the cat, who on any given day grazes on grass,
pounced back to sliding door begging for couch comfort,
wind chiming backyard bells, ferocious in warning.

are we all category four,
circling somewhere over the Atlantic and hoping to make landfall
before dusk, before the energies we coalesce
curl centripetal and dissipate into dark skies
that threaten thunder but deliver nothing?   you

who were the eye of the storm
in every letter of the alphabet, you were the big one
each of us remembers, your path elliptical and
vectored electronically as on TV maps and over
tomatoes that continue to ripen on vines
in this September garden, where it is still raining

swallow *(verb)*

is this why i propped cellphone against
the old answering machine to record
your left-behind scratch, set down when
you still expected my teenaged child
to call, when a woman alone raising
daughters was still difficult for you to swallow

and me, not wanting my daughter to
press play, not wanting her to stutter,
choke on unexpectedness, your sandpaper voice

me, daughter, unable to loosen myself
from how an illness burdens a soul
with stones

umbilical

… with a child comes death. Death slinks into your mind. It circles your
growing body, and once your child has left it, death circles him too.
—**Claudia Dey,** "Mothers as the Makers of Death", *Paris Review, 2018*

did you wonder when i was born, about death, umbilical cord
wrapping itself around both our necks and separating us from
oxygen, from sodium-coloured hospital light? each impregnation
a double helix, timer set. a vegetable seed sown, flower emerges,
fruit deteriorates under lack of rain or sun or becomes ripe, energy
to feed another life-force. throughout my daughter's birth, death:
electrodes on a cap attached in utero to her head, oxygen mask
sucked, desperate for nutrients. at the moment of your death, she
who was not present at your birth sowing, trailing soft green words
to the air in search of lattices

wild turkey

not even tadpoles in marshy mere, though it was May and we
swatted flies with bare hands beside still lily pads that hovered,
vacant, while green reeds like snorkels filtered brackish water, and
as if amphibian non-attendance could be measured, we waited,
wondered if effluent had seeped into sleeping pool, discussing all
the possibilities of absence before we marched to our car parked
in the small lot that butted up against empty field where a wild
turkey jerked its gait towards a fence of cedars, fragrant barrier of
trees that would soon enough ring newly-built suburban houses,
the line from our nature guidebook lingering in our minds like
odd perfume that arises out of sewage: *Introduced birds adapting
very well to being near people**

*The italicized line is from Roger Tory Peterson and Virginia Marie Peterson's *A Field
Guide to the Birds of Eastern and Central North America.* 5th ed. Boston: Houghton
Mifflin, 2002.

today the earth is damp with scent

after a moonlight of rain, after thunder and lightning bore snow and water, birthed musty lichens on trees behind the house like uterine lining   spongy   thick, on the already ant-riddled soil, a fungal mesh as in the belly you were born with, an iridologist once said, scanning eyes like cartographer, a map of irises, bulbs framed and reframed in concentric circles that carry their own acidity, humus

and the ground today, wet with night's turn to plangent rain pungent, dank as smell of death that attends birth, porous as sac, as membrane expunging continents,   breaks   unearths marrowed remains, succulent in dampness, and redolent, heat aspiring

visitations (echoes)

robin   *ghiandaia*

jay   *merlo, merlo*

)

passero

storno   *gull*   *gull*   *gull*

gabbiano   *pichi*

jay   *corvo*   *gabbiano*

gabbiano   *pichi*

robin   *ghiandaia*

miimii   *finch*

pettirosso   *sparrow*

ghiandaia   *corvo*

finch   *miimii*   *uccello*

gwiingwiish

uccello   *uccello*   *passero*

gyaashkshenh   *uccello*

pettirosso   *gwiingwiish*   *storno*

gwiingwiish

ghiandaia   *corvo*   *corvo*

merlo   *gabbiano*

storno   *gyaashkshenh*   *gabbiano*

uccellino, ino,   ino   ino

aceddhu,   *-ddhu   -ddhu*

processing oxygen

imagine the body as a husk   processing oxygen

so that even   thought   is a side-effect of anaerobic
swallowing aerobic cells

mitochondrial.   life's building blocks hang yellow

crisp cold in November air as leaves that have ceased
producing chlorophyll   that have ceased.

a body wrings its sugars into nucleotides
as deciduous trees fix nitrogen

we are limbless without the oaks

without the sap of maples that sticks to us,
transforms into jewel-like amber.

if the body is a husk, what is a tree?

a planet built on the edge of bacteria

morphs into full-blown fungi that flourish
inside   outside roots of a forest floor

mycorrhizals, for whom the birch and fir,
like human bodies, depend on carbon.

tree bark is a skin that bristles at the sound of sawing

a cut into flesh turns the oxygen of blue blood into red.

imagine the mind tangible as a spider's silk
so gossamer it shines only in the right light,

and weaves a finite space between the air of two trees
as between two persons,

the quality of that silk, the strength of its weft,
the path the spider of the mind travels across that thread

to wait for nourishment,
so precise   so breakable

*Ideas about aerobic and anaerobic cells from "Creating a Better Leaf" by Elizabeth
Kolbert, The New Yorker, December 13, 2021, and mycorrhizals from *Finding the
Mother Tree* by Suzanne Simard (2020)

Water is

quicksilver, changing fates
water is trilobites and arthropods

is fresh awakening
the rain that awaits
the ends of sunny days

water is friend
to mold and holds
the larvae

water   is ocean and is seas
is elemental because it
calls us back to ourselves

water is open and water is closed

is spiritual because it cleanses
water nurtures sunlight in its fingers
turning rays to apple blossoms
floating on waves

water dies and rises again, a splash
a burble as a child's laugh
water to water and rain to rain
we aren't dust or clay, we melt

we are

water, and as such we float
through lives we think are
sediment, but we

water at play is water
is the bear splashing salmon
and she the bearer of water

cucumis sativus

cold   I glare at my lover the sun
      wet

      why have I been left to die, submit to my own decay?
      I asked to grow, perform my duties, turn green my prickles.
                  warmer   sunlight
            white-grey   the squirrels. birds peck
                        sunlight   stubble
serrated edges   my seeds burst but find no fertile ground
                              ser - rated
            I am open, ancient. Observe my skin:
stalks stubble stubble   flower
      to melt is also my duty, to allow my flesh to fester
      to a universe of flies that attend my wake. they drone.
      stubble   leaves
        bees buzz, their words of no consequence
water water   stubble
      tendrils   stubble   yellow
  flowers   on
        I am solitary
      fruit   thick-skinned
        and while I grew, I grew apart, greeted only by
        the earth that expected me, the air and soft rain that caressed my
                        stalks   fruit
                  cheek.   fruit
      Tendrils   squirrel   water
curl, curl,   curl stake   curl
        my flesh is speckled now,
                  stubble   petiole, funnel
      and should a worm, a crawling insect slide its way to sleep

fruit   squirrel   fruit fruit   insect stubble

        inside me should I be content? be leased

        to those who would rent

    water   water water water

      trellis   fence   pole

water   water   fly   unfurl

space inside my peel? my walls are cavernous cool,

curl   light

made lucid by spent green that yet surrounds them

like you, I am a comfortable bed.

water   water   leaves leaves flower

    insect   worms

I shed my skin to the wandering skies

flowerstubble   water

flower   sssssssssseeeeeeeeeeeeeeeeeeeeeeeeeeds

rain

to fall is to have lived at great height,
from edge of stratosphere, caught
between numinous
and ordinary

to have lived at any height
is to have breathed life
to wet earth
is to spatter bones

swell up flesh, submerge
new and old
blue waters in droplets

to condense is to
relinquish vapour, to be
caught on the lamina
of upturned leaf and tubed,
drawn by digitalis, after downpour

to balance on petals is
to have viewed rainbows,
a stop
so temporary before
the rivers of absorption
soak up all dreams

to dream is to net
waters, is to dream
stillness as deluge,
as wind creases and ripples
a dark, sleeping pond

in metamorphosis

the Buddha says everything changes:

spring light widens into evening,
snow falls,   melts,   falls
again, a caterpillar chews through
leaves, becomes sole occupant
of chrysalis as if taking back
misspoken words, transforming
broken clause from turgid grub into
yellow-dotted fritillary fleetness

in metamorphosis, speech opens,
thoughts are butterflied,
and eye and silent tongue in mouth
traverse a poem's lines as silk creates
a texture of words, weaving

every thing changes. things become
non-things become no-thing become
nothing, not, knot.

like a butterfly, orchid sepals spread wide as if to spin

fall to windswept earth, mingle with dust and milkweed

thirst

there's a longing for 's' the 'th' makes,

      voiceless, which is what we become in the absence of water

i like to think that before birth, we were diacritical

                hanging mid-air, attached to thought

and that the ink of flesh printed us,

        commas swimming in the rush of amniotic fluids

        drought   is immense,   a desert dreaming of oasis

or singular as winter,   water trapped into crystal fields

   that open   wide unto themselves,   the crunch of meaning

      that's what birth is, washing off vernix

within *thirst*, the sole vowel, '*i*':

'*r*'- hooked like a fish, tugged

to the end of its line, mouthing consonants

wind

I carry portent   as gale
in the sway of a branch,
breaking

am a twist west,
drop showers on waking dawn,
am in love

with myself, flick
my hand, a sweep
unsettling dust,

my tongue a language
incomprehensible
(I enjoy my diversions).

I mutter
profanities your ears do not hear –
you feel my slap, then

my caress   oh the sweetness
of your arm. I am not
so cold as not to cool

you under summer sun and yet
I turn, your axis blurs,
sirocco moon crinkles stars

the winds have come

and with them the rational light
has shifted, turning
the Japanese maple in the garden
golden, turning turning

as if a line from Ecclesiastes
was a thread
that could stitch us to this shift
and sew:

a season
a measurement
a notional changing trick of light into
a song
a boat with mast
a sail to fasten souls to

the canopy, canvas
above the gentle rocking
of the garden's swinging bench
              is flapping

sciuris carolinensis

worms scavenge for meaning. meaning is, meaning yours
like bodies. my body is concrete

pour that space. raze day.
day will habituate for you my habits

blessed, have you been thinking forest?
growth is old within me

bury me not, but do.
splinters. a tree's too close

am I then even your wooden fence?
against me a predator

call me forever

will birds name my existence?
you will forget to become my flag

see your eyes, nations, all colours
so that fallen leaves newly dead under me

instead will bury me a tail on fur,
a spindly climb feels too cold across

shingles, rooftops, a shaft. scurry,
no apologies for you were not born to steal,

to make such delicious tomatoes grow.
I make it my right to leave a heart larger than

myself left half-eaten. that is the meaning of soul

shortened limbs to buried appendages.
beneath a tree I am tall, decaying

bury me flattened there, my likeness seen
to have been by the road, snowed

I am heavy under burial

visitations (osso)

femur   liver   hypothalamus   ovary

toe   Giuseppina Caterina/ Catina *ligament   salivary gland   tibia   diaphragm*

Lucrezia   *corpuscle*   *Giuseppina*

ulna   Adriana   *radius   tendon   optic*

nerve   pharynx   Rosalbina   *trachea   malleus   esophagus*

hinocchio   tarsal   stapes

Lucrezia   aorta   tricep   bronchiole

cilia   corpus   callosum   cervix   Rosalbina

Adriana   epiglotti   sternum   ventricle

endometrium   Adriana   uvula   ghamba

Maria Teresa   *nostril   cochlea*

calf   larynx capo   ankle   Giuseppina
Adriana   gallbladder   Lucrezia

coccyx   spinal cord   retina   pelvis   plasma

Rosalbina   temporal lobe   central nervous system

Adriana   basal ganglia   panza

bone marrow   Rosalbina   platelets

occipital lobe   sclera   eye   Adriana

pedi   septum   pre-frontal cortex   red blood cells

metatarsal   anus   kidney

iris

preparing to overwinter

after you died, they sent a bouquet

pink and white flowers with a bow
lilies, large stargazers

to make us look beyond their stamens, up
to the heavens where they said you would go

though I had viewed you
through curls cut against my will

through feet in black patent that no matter the size
wore themselves tightly.

when we threw the flowers out, it was cold
though the snow hadn't yet flown

petals tossed on dead remains of garden
yellowed tomato stalks, blackened leaves of basil

we mulched
the petals in wet soil

returning a part of you
to earth

leftover precipitation

in winter you can build an ice castle

replete with walls and turret,
transform leftover precipitation

the way birds transform fallen leaves,
twigs, settle nests high up in the trees.

we don't build easily from scraps.

instead, we cultivate stronger crops
and clear, engineer new fruit we sow
deep in potash-driven soil.

when it snows, children shelter stocks
of snowballs inside their forts, roll

snow figures taller than themselves
and carve their own images, angels
beneath body's weight.

we adults watch from behind double-glazed storm windows

where the blue of shadowed crystals
molds into low walls we no longer see

across the expanse of snow, between
homes and playing children, a desert.

a cardinal on a spare branch calls to its mate

snow

we, the miraculous ones,

are the visitors, who drift to horizon and spin
half-light blues in planetary orbit,
over everything

we attach, detach

while you dream of tall hills
and colours that burn through covered lights
which we shower with our blessings.

sun readies us to sparkle;
we surrender silver into melting pools

into midnight, lullabies in the shushing

of snowshoed feet across fields, down
the slow drip, glaciation

into icicles,
each different, each the same

we, the numberless, the cloud-cast

infinite snow-hair, lash-wipe
floating onto tongues, stinging

blizzard

even the trees bend in a blizzard

the thrashing snow and ice pellets,
the blurred vision.

if you'd been an elephant,
you'd have marched through mountain passes,

split the storm, carved your path,
Red Sea of winter.

(i'm not that mighty. i fear the elements,
their lashes, fierce against my safe window.)

you never avoided a show

carried your banners like an entourage
so citizens laid down their palms before you.

but you're not an elephant, there are no trumpets,

the snow and ice are meaningless,
the birds silent.

now, i watch the weather, its bands of red
in Doppler. and storm closures,

a havoc you would have trampled

after the obit

I always knew that grief was
something I could smell.
—**Victoria Chang,** *OBIT*

the way a half-rotten tomato smells
when you slice down its middle

the meanness of spores invading
soft, red flesh as stipples curled
during blanching to remove tomato husks,
so readily is skin permeable.

when a cell dies, it's not a conquest,
it's a shedding

each fragrance stripped from the body
as paint layers that slip
out of their semi-gloss, their eggshells

removing polish requires a thinner

which is how the body appears, in collapse

death exudes its own scent, but grief

is sensed in colognes wafting
from darkly-dressed handshakes,
in the cups of too strong coffee

in the first time you make tomato sauce,
sense your mother's absent hands
in the aroma of tomatoes stewing

the garden sleeps now

under a blueness scrubbed
of wanting

scrubbed of the rhizome that once arched
towards another dawn, the light

plates gold
on anything that catches light

now, an upper window flashes
silence to the cold before

blue ground lies down,
gives way to the rooted

spectacle of earth, dark
absented of shadows

definition

from the Oxford dictionary of current English, **silhouette** /ˌsɪluːˈet/ – **n. 1** picture showing the outline only, usu. in black on white or cut from paper. **2** dark shadow or outline against a lighter background.

after all the digging, of what remains on the surface

d fin t on

fr m the O f d icti nary f cur e t ng ish, **si ho et e** /,sIlu:'et/ **n. 1**
a p ctu e sh w g the utl n on y, usu. in b a k on hi e cut f om pa e
. **2** d r s ad ow or utl ne agai s a l ghte b ck ro d.

                               aft r all   , wh t re ains on t e s rf ce

and Binding

Of the first part

What is a visitation?

This was a question I posed, or which was posed to me, by a bird, rabbit, the fly that landed on my arm, the butterfly that willingly paused on a shrub in the summer of 2020. That it was the first summer of the Covid lockdowns you already know. That so many of us engaged in new questions, new sets of questions, a fact with some relevance. I mention the date as a kind of scene setting.

I lost my mother four months prior to the pandemic. 'Losing' a term with little relevance as the life of another person is never ours to possess.

What is a loss?

In nature, there is loss and life, each new day. Throughout the pandemic, there have been deaths, and a fight for life. I sat in my backyard in the summer of 2020. Death all around, and also rebirth. A cycle palpable, visible. Quotidian.

"Visitation" describes the ritual of bearing witness. I visit a funeral home to pay homage to an embalmed body. I bear witness, bear grief as a gift, an offering to deceased spirits. Ghosts possess the power of visitation, as in dreams where my mother still visits me.

We are all visitors. In the garden there are animals, plants, the soil, rain. We are visitors in a world that continues its exertions, regardless of our presence.

In the summer of 2020, I began to imagine what it might be like to be an eastern cottontail rabbit, a worm, a tomato on the vine, ripening. I wondered: what is the language a maple speaks? What might an onion say, or snow falling, or a grasshopper? What language could I use to inhabit those imagined spaces? How have we constructed language to capture the macrocosm that exists in the space of a backyard garden?

What is the language of nature? In a world altering as a result of climate change, what is it about nature we have worked so hard to ignore, to miss?

I wanted to identify the birds. They flew in and out of my garden and my attempts to place them were fruitless, the descriptions of bird calls too subjective in my view for me to latch on to anything more than the call of a chickadee. I examined wing bars, the meaning of rufous breast, the shape of tail feathers. Birds too as visitors.

I couldn't write a poem from the perspective of a bird. Birds wanted to fly in and out of the manuscript (at least in my imagination), signaling their inaccessibility, their visitations, the multiplicity of those visitations, unnumbered, unordered, a movement towards randomness. Later, I read Catherine Graham's words in *AEther: an out of body lyric:* "What makes the bird / the natural symbol for liminal expression? / / *They have learned how to move without being grounded.*"

The birds in my book are not grounded. Like us, they are visitors, and their "visitations" multiple. The first of these "visitations" sequences lists the birds in alphabetic order. In the Linnaean system of classification, plants and animals are known by their binomial structure, species and variety. Those names called to me for disruption, to mimic indistinguishable chatter, to mimic the disorientation so many of us felt during the first wave of the pandemic. To mimic my vertigo after losing my mother. How to describe the messiness when we lose classificatory systems?

What is the meaning of a classification?

I love the sound of Latin. Perhaps I love it because it is the proto-language of Italian, the language of my parents, grandparents, my family. No, not Italian. Calabrese. And somewhere in my history, Sicilian. I've read that Calabrese and other southern dialects descended directly from Latin itself. I imagine Latin merging with the languages spoken by the Sicels, or the Brutti. Should I trace my linguistic roots directly from Latin?

They say that Latin is a dead language.

Latin, the supposedly "universal" classificatory language. I make no claims for universality.

We live in a world where we are only now beginning to understand the consequences of classifying. Only now are we in the West waking up to decolonize our minds, our languages, our actions. While my poetic ear resonated with the sounds of words like *Dissosteira carolina*, it was also attuned to the act of disrupting these Latin classifications, splitting their binomial names into retroreflective signs, rendering them airborne.

We don't know what birds would call themselves. I have rendered their names in Latin, in English, in Italian, in Calabrese, in Anishinaabemowin. I am a settler, and these poems are situated within, and were written on the Lands of the Great Mississauga Nations. These Nations are signatories to the Williams Treaties, and include the Mississaugas of Scugog Island First Nation, First Nations of Alderville, Beausoleil, Curve Lake, Hiawatha, Chippewas of Georgina Island, and Rama. A local history book from my public library tells me that where I live was once a farm owned by a settler. I know that story is colonial history. I know this backyard that frames my poems has a history that goes back for millennia, a history that is not mine to tell. Languages tell their own stories, and in the "visitations" sequences, I hope to honour this garden's first storytellers, and their continued and future stories by making visible the first language these birds heard, as I humbly offer my own.

What I call "my" yard is not "mine". It is a place where I sit from spring to fall. It is a place bounded by a wooden fence that was erected before I moved here, before I too took up stewardship of this place.

All boxes we live in can be made of wood, the greens and browns the eye attempts to pin down.

Visitations captured through an optic nerve.

Morphology is a word that means "the study of the forms of things, especially plants and animals". What is the form of a word? of language? of a book? A rabbit warren, a bird's nest, the spread of underground roots. What is the form of a species that studies and writes books? Page turning, right to left and left to write, *right*. A Freudian slip in the direction of print. A written page like a field being ploughed, and a pen and its relation to the silent tongue in the mouth, the tongue, *lingua*, of language.

***

In other words, two

The poems in this collection are doubles, mirrors. The poet speaks of nature, and nature responds, nature corrects. Nature as imagined by the poet. They dance together, the poet and nature, throughout these pages, intertwined, a double helix like the twists of an umbilical cord floating in amniotic fluid. The unexpected turns, the meaning of absence and the composition of futurity.

Meaning is an accordion that doubles back on itself. A book is an object held in the mind. Dionne Brand asserts: "Writing is an act of desire, as is reading." What do you desire from these pages? What does the poet desire for you to know? What does the slippery paper of a daffodil sheaf communicate to itself or to the plants around it?

Some of the poems in this collection are centred in the middle of the page, a sign that the imagined voice of the onion, the carrot, the grasshopper is bounded by the margins of what is knowable and what is not. There is much to be annotated in the space surrounding nature-voiced poems.

Where it is clear the trope of the poet as speaker operates, these poems sit on the left margin as per typical writing conventions. The poet acknowledges the leash of language that binds us to our edges.

This collection of poems comes complete with a glossary, or a gloss, which is an overview, a tongue touching its own teeth.

The poet believes her fascination with language derives from the fact that her grandfather was born in a town called *Linguaglossa*, both *lingua* in Latin (or Italian) and *glossa* in Greek meaning tongue.

She has written about this elsewhere, in another poem, in another collection. She allows these tongues to become part of her mythology.

For after all, what is a mythos if not a voice or its spirit inside the trunk of a tree, awaiting release?

Sources

For many of the Latin animal and plant names: Wikipedia, Roger Tory Peterson and Virginia Marie Peterson's *A Field Guide to the Birds of Eastern and Central North America*. 5th ed. Boston: Houghton Mifflin, 2002, *Hinterland Who's Who*, https://www.hww.ca/en/wildlife/mammals/-eastern-grey-squirrel.html, Orthoptera of Ontario https://orthoptera.ca/index.php?location=-Ontario&rank=order&name=Orthoptera

For definitions and translations: the Oxford English Dictionary, the Collins English – Italian/ Italian-English Dictionary, for Calabrese translations, Dialettando.com (https://www.dialettando.-com), the online Nishnaabemwin dictionary: https://dictionary.nishnaabemwin.atlas-ling.ca/ and Ontario Parks website, https://www.ontarioparks.com/parksblog/introduction-to-anishinaabe-mowin/

Glossary

(Note: where the language is unspecified, it is Latin)

Aceddhu (Calabrese) – bird
Acer saccharum – a sugar maple
Archilocus colubris – ruby-throated hummingbird
Agelaius phoeniceus – red-winged blackbird
Cardinalis cardinalis – northern cardinal
Carduelis pinus – pine siskin
Carduelis tristis – American goldfinch
Carolina dissosteira – Carolina grasshopper
Carpodacus mexicanus – house finch
Carpodacus purpureus – purple finch
Corvo (Italian) – a crow
Corvus brachyrhyncos – American crow
Cucumis sativus – cucumber
Danaus plexippus – a monarch butterfly
Formiche (Italian) – ants
Gabbiano (Italian) – seagull
Ghiandaia (Italian) – a jay
Gwiingwiish (Anishnaabemowin) – a jay
Gyaashkshenh (Anishnaabemowin) – a seagull
Junco hyemalis – dark-eyed ("slate-colored") junco
Larus delawarensis – herring gull
Lepidoptera – butterflies
Lumbricus – a worm
Merlo – blackbird
Miimii (Anishnaabemowin) – a pigeon
Passer domesticus – house sparrow
Passero (Italian) – a swallow
Pettirosso (Italian) – a robin

Pichi (Anishnaabemowin) – a robin
Poecile atricapilla – black-capped chickadee
Quiscalus quiscula – common grackle
Sciuris carolinensis – a squirrel
Solanum lycopersicum – a roma tomato
Spizella passerina – chipping sparrow
Spizella pusilla – field sparrow
Storno – starling
Sturnus vulgaris – European starling
Sylvilagus floridanus – eastern cottontail rabbit
Turdus migratorius – American robin
Uccelli (Italian) – birds
Zenaida macroura – mourning dove

Acknowledgements

"a day is as long as" and "MIXED-METHODS EXPERIMENTAL STUDY OF ACER SACCHARUM IN SITU, WITH PROGNOSIS BY ARBORISTS AND LINGUISTS ON THE FUTURE OF INTERSPECIES COMMUNICATION: AN INVESTIGATION"
first published in *The /tɛmz/ Review*, issue seventeen, December 2021, available at: https://www.thetemzreview.com/
"in the garden" was first published in *Fresh Voices*, League of Canadian Poets, June 2020
"in metamorphosis" won 2nd prize in the 2022 Carmen Ziolkowski Poetry Prize run by Lawrence House
"preparing to overwinter" first appeared in *The Wild Word*, "Winter Song" Issue #56, December 2020, available at: https://thewildword.com/
"your town" first published in *The Windsor Review*, issue 55. No. 1, Fall 2021
"Water is" first published in *The Beliveau Review*, issue 1, available at: https://beliveaubooks.wixsite.com/home
"weirding" first published in *Dr. Drummond Poetry Contest Anthology*, 2021

My sincere thanks:

to Anna Van Valkenburg and my editor and publisher Michael Mirolla at Guernica Editions for all their generous help and support, and for bringing this book to print;

to Errol F. Richardson, who designed the book's cover and turned my vision into reality;

to Jordan Abel, my outstanding instructor at the Sage Hill Writing Experience's 2021 Summer Writing Intensive where I first workshopped the manuscript for this book. That experience shaped the direction of this work, and completely transformed how I understand poetry. I am forever grateful for having had the opportunity to learn from you about all that poetry can be;

to Karen Solie, Di Brandt, and Kate Marshall Flaherty for their respective workshops, out of which several of these poems were written;

to Allan Briesmaster, for his willingness to share his expertise, generosity and feedback in helping me fine tune the manuscript before I sent out queries;

to the larger poetry and writing community, in person and online, who in big and small ways nurture me on this poetry journey;

to all the Annex Writing Circle folks, especially Lee Parpart, Ariane Blackman, Genevieve Chornenki, Njoroge Mungai, June Rogers, Ed Seaward, Stephanie Wyeld, and Pamela Yuen-Elkerbout, who read and provided feedback on earlier drafts of several these poems. I'm fortunate to be a member of your circle;

to the Moonsammys and Martones, for their support and that really intense debate over which cover image to choose!;

to friends for their support of my writing and for shared laughter: Jesse Dorsay and Angela Porter, Hyacintha Lord, Sonia Senior-Martin, Gwen Tuinman, and especially Jennifer Sorensen;

and most of all, to my family: Bronwyn, Maeve, and Raj, you are the spine, the stitching, the glue, the cover and content of my story. What can I say? *Con tanto affetto.*

About the Author

Born in Toronto and currently a Durham Region resident, **Renée M. Sgroi** is the author of one previous poetry collection, *life print, in points* (erbacce-press) and the editor of the poetry anthology, *Written Tenfold* (Poetry Friendly Press). A member of the League of Canadian Poets, The Writers' Union of Canada, the Canadian Authors Association, the Association of Italian-Canadian Writers, The Ontario Poetry Society, and a contributing editor for *Arc Poetry Magazine*, Renée's poems have been published in *Literary Review of Canada, Pinhole Poetry, The Windsor Review, the /tɛmz/ review, The Prairie Journal, Poetry Pause* and numerous anthologies. Find her online: reneemsgroi.com

Printed by Imprimerie Gauvin
Gatineau, Québec